Poole

in old picture postcards

by
Mary M. Davenport

European Library - Zaltbommel/Netherlands MCMLXXXVI

For Diana and Susan

GB ISBN 90 288 3361 7 / CIP

European Library in Zaltbommel/Netherlands publishes among other things the following series:

IN OLD PICTURE POSTCARDS *is a series of books which sets out to show what a particular place looked like and what life was like in Victorian and Edwardian times. A book about virtually every town in the United Kingdom is to be published in this series. By the end of this year about 300 different volumes will have appeared. 1,500 books have already been published devoted to the Netherlands with the title* **In oude ansichten.** *In Germany, Austria and Switzerland 650, 100 and 25 books have been published as* **In alten Ansichten;** *in France by the name* **En cartes postales anciennes** *and in Belgium as* **In oude prentkaarten** *and/or* **En cartes postales anciennes** *150 respectively 400 volumes have been published.*

For further particulars about published or forthcoming books, apply to your bookseller or direct to the publisher.

This edition has been printed and bound by Grafisch Bedrijf De Steigerpoort in Zaltbommel/Netherlands.

INTRODUCTION

Do you remember the islands
Set in a sunlit sea,
The busy quay with masted ships,
Where we dreamed eternally.

Poole, like its name, is a peaceful place, with a great deal of exciting history hidden in its old streets, and in the fine merchants houses now restored to their former glory. This is a seaport known to mariners throughout the ages, for Poole harbour has always been a safe haven for ships running from the Channel storms. Almost an inland sea, seven miles long and more than half as wide, this blue lagoon of Dorset is one of the most beautiful sights at any season of the year.

Today, Poole has blossomed into a holiday resort with a distinctly maritime air, the Quay always busy with trading ships loading and unloading, visiting yachts from many countries, and leisure craft scudding across the waters of the harbour.

This was a landing place in the 10th century for the pirate hordes of the Norsemen. King Canute sailed into the harbour in 1015 with his fleet bound for Wareham. Poole's first charter was granted in 1248 by the crusader William Longspée, Lord of the Manor of Canford. In the reign of Henry III the town was a depot for provisioning his fleet. In the 14th century Poole sent four ships to the seige of Calais. By 1433 the town became a Port of the Staples by order of Henry VI.

Like many ports in the West Country the town's most prosperous time was during the reign of Queen Elizabeth I and this continued on into the 19th century.

Men of vision and vigour became wealthy merchants, sending their ships to trade in fish, wool and timber in far-flung countries. Newfoundland became an important link, many of the men had been seamen in the fishing ships sailing from Poole, they became captains and owned their own ships, they built splendid houses in the High Street, and great mansions outside the town.

There was trade with Spain, the West Indies, the Americas and Canada. Since many ships were built in Poole they were also provisioned here and from nearby villages, so other trades flourished.

Into the harbour on 16th August 1830 sailed the English Packet boat 'Great Britain', on board was the dethroned King of France, Charles X and his family, they landed on the quay and found refuge at Lulworth Castle. In the 19th century Poole Park was marshland at the edge of Parkstone Bay, when the railway embankment was built in 1872 it cut off part of the bay and left a saltwater lake. How the Poole Council of the day were able to develop the park is fascinating history of which I write in later pages. The park was opened by H.R.H. Edward, Prince of Wales, in 1890.

On the Quay are many ancient inns and the impressive Poole Pottery building; it still retains the original wall dating from the 19th century. Pottery has been made in Poole since Roman times, the clay found in the area is some of the finest in the world. The delightful Museum of Poole Pottery Ltd. will take you through the many processes to the finished product, it is a delight to visit.

As the years of the 19th century passed the fortunes of many Poole merchants were lost through a decline in trade, particularly fish. Gradually the fine houses in the old town were left empty, they deteriorated, some were lost altogether through neglect, until in 1975 the Council of Europe designated that year as European Architectural Heritage Year, and the area of the old town of Poole was chosen as one of the four projects in the United Kingdom to be conserved and enhanced.

The result is a constant joy to all who visit it today, and for those who live there. The restored great family houses and the cottages where the ships masters and craftsmen once lived are again the homes of caring people, with the Parish Church of St. James full of many treasures to delight the eye.

Beyond the 'town within a town' is the busy bustling hub of Poole, the finest music, art and drama are to be found here.

Poole today is a lively place, catering for those who love the beauty of days past, and for the young and old alike who are forever looking forward.

Acknowledgements

I am most grateful to the many people who have so kindly and generously helped me in compiling this book. In particular I wish to thank Mr. L.H. Hayward, Curator of the Poole Pottery Museum, for giving me so many details of old Poole; Mrs. J. Beauchamp; Mr. and Mrs. J.R. Brady of Compton Acres; Mr. A. Bromby, Mr. T.P. Burr, the National Trust, Wessex; Mr. and Mrs. B. Dutton, Mrs. L. Poole, Mr. G. Whiting, and the John Lewis Partnership; Poole Pottery Ltd.; Mrs. S.J. Griffths, The Royal National Lifeboat Institution; Mr. F. Ramsbottom; the Reverend A. Woodley; and my husband for his invaluable assistance.

1. A photograph of the Quay showing how it must have looked at the turn of the century. The forest of masts indicate the large number of sailing vessels in the harbour. There was much activity in the town and the neighbourhood for the manufacture of rope, twine and sailcloth, as well as the big tile industry. Looking westward note the Seamen's Institute, two granaries and the Poole Arms Inn.

2. A cameo of this almost landlocked harbour. If followed closely it would be almost one hundred miles around, with islands, and many channels through the shallow mud flats, these dry out at low tide. At high tide there is a four hour stand. Undoubtedly one of the finest natural harbours in the world, it has been the centre of trading activity since Roman times. As the river Frome began to silt up in the 13th century, Poole became the more important port for trading ships, since they could no longer reach Wareham.

3. Hamworthy Bridge with the Poole coat of arms in the corner, circa 1910. A busy trading area, vessels bringing in coal and timber, china clay from Cornwall for the potteries, and loading up with animal feeding stuffs and malt barley. This was once the ancient port of Moriconium, excavations uncovered the site of an early Iron Age village. The Romans were here in the first century, and many relics have been unearthed. A new church has been built to replace the earlier St. Michael's Church. The large mound in the old churchyard is of interest for here were buried soldiers of the Parliamentary forces who fell at Poole. Oliver Cromwell stayed at the old rectory, as did the Duke of Wellington. The rectory was built around 1610; it has now been added to the nearby school.

4. Poole High Street in the early part of the century, with a splendid view of the Methodist Church. The architect for the present church, built in 1880, was Charles Bell and the builders Samuel Clarke. The cost of the building was £7,036, and by 1884 the debt had been reduced to £1,250 and this was cleared by 1901. The church is built of Somerset black rock with Bath stone dressings. The pillars are made of polished Shap granite. The acoustics are excellent within the building. The spire is 90 feet high and before the erection of various high flats in the Old Town was a landmark for sailors. When it was first built Mr. Caleb Snook and a group of young men climbed up the tower and sang hymns.

5. High Street, Poole. The Longfleet Post Office was kept by Mr. C.T. Snook, who was also a newsagent and stationer. Later the business passed to his son, Mr. Ewart Snook. Note the ground length dresses of the shoppers, the little boys wearing knickerbockers, and the pedestrians casually crossing the road. This part of the High Street no longer exists, for today the ground is covered by the Arndale Shopping Centre.

6. A rare photograph of the busy Quay. Of particular interest is the railway line running along the edge of the Quay enabling ships to be easily loaded and unloaded. Through the centuries this has been a working harbour as it is today. There is always great activity here, ships from many nations call from all parts of the world, as well as leisure craft that have made long voyages.

7. A view of the harbour looking across to the quay, postmarked 1904. During the summer every third year the ancient tradition of Beating the Bounds of Poole Harbour is made by the Admiral of the Port, the Mayor and his party and a jury of watermen. At certain points along the route an old charter is read, claiming jurisdiction 'over land, water, fish and folk'.

8. Postmarked 1904 this peaceful scene is but a short walk from the quay and the town. The park comprises of 100 acres of landscaped gardens and lakes. Originally, in the Victorian era Poole Council had purchased from Lord Wimborne 20 acres of land between Ladies Walking Field and Kingland Road, with the scheme of making it into a park and recreation ground, but it was later decided it was not suitable for this purpose. The Council had paid one hundred pounds for the site and they then applied to Lord Wimborne to buy land to the north of Parkstone Bay. Imagine their pleasure, when he said he was happy to give them the site they required on condition that it was laid out as a park and recreation ground, and maintained for the inhabitants forever.

9. The Freshwater Lake, Poole Park, as seen in 1907. Many varieties of duck have found a good feeding ground here, including the mandarins, red-crested pochard, rosybills and the familiar tufted ducks.

10. Known as the Town Hall up to 1904 this fine Georgian building has many unusual features. It is one of Poole's most beautiful buildings, the graceful flights of spiral steps meet under the limestone portico. The building is of red brick with arcading below. On the top of the building is a cupola. Of interest are the old shop fronts and the donkey and cart.

11. This grand Victorian building was at one time the Free Library, School of Art and Museum in Mount Street, it was built between 1887 and 1890. The Library was opened in 1887. It was the gift of J.J. Norton, a timber and slate merchant, and it commemorates Queen Victoria's Jubilee. At the time the project aroused a great deal of controversy. This card was sent by my aunt and is postmarked 1904. Today there is a new Library in the Arndale Centre and this old building has been put to commercial use, whilst still retaining its façade.

12. The ancient thatched cottage said to date from the sixteenth century stood on the corner of the High Street and Carter's Lane. The lane is still there running back to Hill Street. Of particular interest are the costumes of the two groups of children watching the photographer. The neat design of the paving stones on the roadway create a pleasing pattern. The Poole coat-of-arms is in the corner.

13. Another view of the old thatched cottage. Here lived Arthur James, the town crier, who was also the town's billposter. The notice in front of the pots of plants in the window reads 'Poole Bill Posting Compy'. The cottage was demolished in 1919.

14. The Custom House is late Georgian in style and was built in 1813, on the site of an Elizabethan building which was destroyed by fire. The fine double flight of steps up to the classical portico are similar to those of the Guildhall in Market Street. The Town Beam standing in front of the Custom House is of great interest, it bears a plaque which reads: *The Baylye or his Deputye shall Receive of every Straunger or ffarinor having goodes or marchandyzes to be wayed, for the paysadze or weighinge the same at the Towne Beame, appointed for that purpose, one halfpennye for every hundred weight, which halfpennye shall be the whole duty as well for the Beame as for the porters and labour for the puttinge in and takinge out.*

15. On this view, postmarked 1905, we see the former Town Hall is now known as the Guildhall. Note the delivery boy wearing knickerbockers and carrying a large basket, also the long dresses of the pedestrians. Today this building is the excellent Guildhall Museum, which houses a great amount of fascinating memorabilia of Poole from the 18th and the 19th centuries.

16. St. Georges Almshouses, first built in the time of Henry V and for a long time the property of St. Georges Guild, they passed to the Crown in 1547 and were purchased by the Corporation in 1550. They are the only Tudor Almshouses in Poole, and have been devoted to the poor for 500 years.

17. The Antelope Hotel is a famous old posting house in the High Street. A popular meeting place through the centuries, it still retains part of the original 15th century building. Situated so conveniently near the quay it was a coaching hostelry for Poole harbour; stables still exist at the rear of the premises where fresh teams of horses were kept ready for the coach service to Bath, Bristol, Southampton, Lymington, Weymouth and London.

18. An interesting scene in Poole Park, with a cricket match in progress, and a good view of the Pavilion. The costumes of the spectators are those of the Edwardian era. Matches were played here throughout the summer months. Today many other amenities have been added, sailing, rowing and childrens pedal craft, also a model yacht enclosure, a popular pastime with the local club.

19. Poole from Constitution Hill. In the foreground may be seen the typical shrubland of the area that once surrounded the whole of the town, and isolated it from other parts of Dorset. It is the property of Poole Corporation and has been left in its natural state. There are wonderful views across the harbour to the Purbeck Hills beyond.

20. A view of Poole from Constitution Hill at the turn of the century. This postcard is postmarked Poole, 1903, it commands a fine panorama of the area, which was a favourite place to visit and to enjoy the countryside.

21. Taken from another angle this shows the harbour from Constitution Hill. The old tram with its open top is of particular interest. We see Brownsea Island and the backdrop of the Purbeck Hills beyond.

22. St. Peter's Church, Parkstone, is very graceful in style. Within the church seven Florentine lamps hang from the chancel roof, and two Venetian candlesticks stand at the top of the sanctuary steps. Lord and Lady Baden-Powell were married here in 1912. The parishioners of St. Peter's made a great contribution to the renovating of St. Mary's Church on Brownsea Island after its years of neglect.

23. A tranquil scene in Parkstone Park. Many fine residences were built here amongst the pine trees, and well-screened from cold winds. The village of Parkstone, as it then was, gained a high reputation as a health resort, on account of its warm and protected environment. It became known as 'The English Mentone' for its mild climate and very low rainfall.

24. The tram terminus will be remembered by many older residents. How peaceful it looks with scarcely any traffic, and the small boy standing in the centre of the street. In 1900 the British Traction Company obtained permission to construct a tramway from Poole to the County Gates, despite there being much opposition from Bournemouth Town Council to the scheme. The line was completed and opened in April 1901. This was one of the first electric tramways to be constructed in the British Isles.

25. A charming old view taken at sunset, showing Poole harbour from Constitution Hill. A pastoral scene with sheep grazing, and the dark purple of the Purbeck Hills beyond. It is said that the hills serve as a rain trap drawing off moisture from the clouds.

26. Ashley Road, Upper Parkstone. The tall building was the public house The Retreat, now demolished. The postcard bears an interesting postmark, Parkstone, 9.45.PM,JY26.06 Dorsetshire.

27. Another view of Ashley Road, Upper Parkstone. The skirts of the shoppers almost sweeping the pavement, the tiny girl wears a frilly white dress and hat, whilst another small girl in a pinafore holds a large hoop. These wooden hoops were made in many sizes, there was a special hoop stick with which to trundle them along. Boys usually had iron hoops.

28. The busy harbour with vessels of every size. The pleasure boats plying for hire advertise a 'Trip round the Island' for 2/6d, children 1/3d, rather more today. Harvey's is an old established pleasure boat business; Mr. Bernard Harvey told me that it was started by his great-grandfather in 1885. A boat trip to Brownsea Island by way of the very beautiful smaller islands is a memorable experience.

29. A joyous scene on Poole quay in the early days of the century. How delightful all the young girls look in their white dresses and large hats. Note the group of fishermen chatting in the foreground. Everyone looks very happy, the sun is shining and there is a feeling of expectation in the air. It is obviously a public holiday, what are they all waiting for?

30. A typical road leading down to the Bay, Sandbanks, the pine tree in the foreground is a splendid example of these great trees that abound here, whilst the sandy tracks have given way to tarmac roads, and well kept gardens with neatly trimmed hedges, as we see in the picture. It is curious to remember that in early Edwardian days this wild and beautiful promontory was for sale for one thousand pounds.

31. The Two Bays, Sandbanks. From here the ferry to Shell Bay is a popular trip; I well remember as a child many happy visits to this shell strewn shore. The Sandbanks to Studland Ferry is a great saving of mileage for motorists, about fifteen miles if you are visiting Wareham. In the 1920's there was a great surge of building as Sandbanks became a favourite place for many business people from Poole to build a second home here.

32. A peaceful scene on the beach, Sandbanks, from Simpson's Folly. Once the haunt of smugglers who landed at Studland and carried their contraband across the bracken and heather to avoid the customs men on the lookout at the harbour entrance. The booty was loaded into flat-bottomed boats at Redhorn Quay, Greenland and Brand's Point. The first Poole lifeboat was housed at Sandbanks, and in 1865 the crew had to be taken from the Antelope Hotel in the High Street to Sandbanks to man the boat.

33. The park of Upton House, this rolling expanse of lawn stretches down to the shores of Holes Bay. It is a peaceful place where residents of Poole and their visitors may stroll and enjoy the beautiful views, since the house and gardens are owned and maintained by Poole Corporation. The Friends of Upton Park arrange many delightful events here to raise funds for its upkeep. In the spring there are drifts of daffodils beneath the trees, many species of birds are found here, and the peacocks parade on the terrace of the old house in the sunshine. The house was built about 1816 by Christopher Spurrier; he was a member of the merchant family who traded from Poole to Newfoundland, and who flourished on this rich trade in the 18th and 19th centuries.

View of Poole Harbour from Compton Acres

34. A view of Poole Harbour from Compton Acres, with the glorious colours of Brownsea Island and the Purbeck Hills in the distance. This fine estate was developed in 1919 as a series of exquisite gardens, evolved from the wild moorland to a place of peace and inspiration. The cost for those days was enormous, around £220,000. Since that time there have been many additions made to the gardens by the present owners, Mr. and Mrs. J.R. Brady. When firs and pines have had to be cut down they have been replaced with many rare specimen trees.

"The Italian Garden", Compton Acres, Canford Cliffs, Poole, Dorset. *Photo: E. Nägele, John Hinde Studios.*

35. The lovely Italian Garden, Compton Acres, with its carved stone fountains and glittering pool, the home of waterlilies and thousands of goldfish. The grass edged borders are filled with tulips and spring flowers, during the summer the borders are planted with annuals in a myriad of colours. The domed 'Temple of Bacchus' is supported on stone pillars, and the 'God of Wine' is finely sculptured in Carrara marble.

36. A beautiful setting for the Palm Court and the Wishing Well, Compton Acres. The well is Venetian and carved from a solid block of stone, the money thrown into the well with a wish is sent to the Victoria Home for Crippled Children and other deserving charities. A very peaceful place to pause a while, and rest on one of the carved marble seats.

37. A scene in the Japanese Garden at Compton Acres, here you find yourself transported to an Oriental world, faithfully constructed by a Japanese architect and his team of workmen from Japan. The sunken lake, the cascade, the bridges and stepping stones all combine with the Temple to create an unforgettable sight. Near the Summer House stands the Goddess who protects children. The ancient figure of Buddha is said to be three thousand years old. How remarkable it is to remember that all this had been wild heathland up to 1919.

38. Some of the beautiful statuary in the Compton Acres Gardens. Many fine pieces have been placed here and the beauty of the sculpture is shown to great advantage by the precise topiary work in the background. A thousand rose bushes flank the paths.

39. If you pass along Canford Cliffs Road today you can hardly imagine that at the turn of the century it was just a rough track, 'Sandy Lane', passing over wild moorland filled with yellow gorse, purple heather and bracken. From the picturesque gorges sprang majestic Scots pines. This postcard is reminiscent of those days, with never a house in sight, only the distant waters of Poole harbour glimpsed through the trees. This area has been preserved in its natural state by the owners, and here in the woodland and sub-tropical glen thrives much unusual flora, a silent, secret place, where nature is king.

40. Branksome Chine at the turn of the century. The postmark is 1907. This delightful spot is little changed, a broad valley winds inland for almost a mile, lined with fine rhododendrons and pine trees, heather and bracken growing along the paths by the stream winding its way to the sea. This picture is dated only by the shadowy figure on the path.

41. The tranquil stream in Branksome Chine, here shady paths bring delightful corners into view, revealing many unexpected scenes. At the beginning of the chine are bowling greens and tennis courts. Once this was bog and swamp, it has been drained without spoiling the natural beauty of the valley.

42. The beach, Branksome Chine, at the turn of the century, a relaxing scene with the quaint bathing machines and square tents, always a feature of any popular beach in Edwardian days. This was once a favourite landing place for smugglers. Notorious was Old Gulliver who operated here into the early part of the 19th century. It is said he kept up to fifty men employed, and owned a fleet of vessels as well as a team of pack horses for conveying his contraband cargoes to London and to many parts of the Midlands.

43. A peaceful view of the promenade and solarium at Branksome Chine. A picturesque and charming corner where the chine ends at the cliff edge with a splendid stretch of sand.

44. Another scene in Branksome Chine, the pines are a feature of the area, heather and wild flowers abound, here in the pine scented air is breathing space, and it is difficult to realise you are so near the busy town. The district around the chine is Branksome Park with a large number of private houses, standing in lovely gardens hidden from view by pines and shrubs. Many of these houses are now hotels and guest houses.

45. The Branksome Tower Hotel, circa 1920. The gardens here were especially delightful and will be remembered by many visitors. The hotel has now been pulled down to make way for a block of flats. Once the mansion of Mr. C.W. Parke, the grounds extended to ten acres. When the house became a hotel it was considered one of the most luxurious on this coast.

46. The SS. Prince of Wales, was one of a fleet of pleasure steamers which sailed along the coast in Edwardian days. They all had familiar names, Balmoral, Lorna Doone, Queen, Solent Queen and they also sailed across to Cherbourg, which must have been quite an event in 1904 when this postcard was sent on 30th June.

47. The SS. Brodick Castle sailed daily from April to October to the Isle of Wight, Brighton, Southampton and Weymouth. The master of the Brodick Castle was for many years Captain Tilsed. On one occasion the steamer sailed from Poole to Brownsea Island with members of the Primrose League, for a garden party at the Castle, by invitation of Mrs. van Raalte. This postcard was sent from Poole by my grandmother, on 12th July 1914.

48. A view taken in the harbour with the quay beyond. Men and ships are always gathered here, and today visitors also are drawn like a magnet to the area, with wonderful views across to Brownsea Island and Sandbanks.

49. Scaplen's Court and its garden have been beautifully preserved, it dates from the 15th century, and is the finest late mediaeval building in the town. During the 18th century it was the home of John Scaplen, a former Sheriff of Poole. By 1900 the building was in a poor state of repair and was condemned. It was in 1924 that Mr. H.P. Smith examined the interior and was able to ascertain that here was a late mediaeval building hidden behind years of added brick and plaster. Many local residents aided by the Town Council of the day and the Society of Poole Men, raised by voluntary subscription sufficent money to restore this historic gem. It was purchased in 1928. Today it is a Museum beautifully furnished in period style.

50. The Winter Parlour, Scaplen's Court. Bath stone has been used for the doorways and windows, the fireplace is of sandstone. The fine ceiling is 16th century, it has had a great deal of restoration, the intersecting beams are of great interest. The windows with their diamond panes allow the sun to glint in fascinating patterns on the old oak within, and on the Dutch floor tiles displayed on the window sill, they are of a green and yellow glaze with which the floor was originally covered.

51. The Solar Room, Scaplen's Court has had an amazing transformation back to its pristine look after being in a sad state as a tenement for many years. The fine collar beam roof shows what the former roof of the Upper Hall must have originally looked like. Above the fireplace the lintel bears the dates 1634 and 1650. The floorboards in the centre of the room are also the original ones. There is some fascinating memorablia on display.

52. A rare postcard of Branksea Castle, or Brownsea as it is known today. The postmark is Poole 1905. The castle was built during the reign of Henry VIII as a coastal defence, and reinforced in the days of Charles I as a defence for Poole. The island stands at the mouth of the harbour, and thus commands all the shipping passing in and out. The castle was held by a Parliamentary garrison during the Civil War, later it became a private home, each new owner making additions to it. Alas, the castle was burnt down in 1896, only the outer walls and Henry VIII's blockhouse in the centre of the castle survived. It was re-built and the interior re-designed.

53. The private landing quay for Brownsea Castle, showing the twin turretted watch towers built by Colonel Waugh, with marble steps at the landing stage, a very imposing approach. We also see the exterior of the Crystal Arcade leading into the gardens, with the castle in the background. Beyond the quay is a delightful small beach with rocks, sand and seaweed, rather like that of a desert island, bushes grow almost to the water's edge, indeed it is easy to transport oneself from civilisation to the peace and quiet of the 19th century, for here nothing has changed.

54. An early picture of Branksea Castle shows what an imposing building it was even before the many structural additions we see today. At one time there was always a guard of six men at the castle whose duty it was to 'watch and ward' the harbour entrance.

55. A pleasing picture of what was then called The New Villa. It shows the well-wooded area and the lake nearby, the habitat of many colonies of rare birds. Today several 'hides' have been established on the island and it is a delight to watch the varied species as they come and go from season to season. From Asia the Sika deer were brought to the island in 1896, adding another interest for the visitors to the castle. Several of the deer swam to the mainland and established a herd near the harbour shore. It is good to know that the Sika have now come back to Brownsea.

56. Brownsea Castle was originally built by Henry VIII as a blockhouse defending the entrance to Poole harbour. It was Sir Humphrey Sturt, Dorset landowner and M.P., who spent large sums of money building the castle in 1765 by raising the blockhouse and adding two wings. In addition he laid out the gardens with hothouses for rare plants. In 1818 Sir Charles Chad bought the island and made many alterations to the interior of the castle. Then in Victorian days came Colonel Waugh who created the fine Tudor style front. In the terrible fire of 1896 many priceless art treasures were lost. Rebuilding began in 1897 and was completed in 1901, Major Kenneth Balfour, the then owner, sold the island to Charles and Florence van Raalte and the golden age of Brownsea began.

57. The unusual 19th century dovecote in the grounds of Brownsea Castle. This Victorian feature had fallen into a poor state and was in danger of disintegration until it was restored by the John Lewis Partnership. These dovecotes were found in all great houses in Victorian days, usually placed in the centre of the yard near the stables. Here we are reminded of R.L. Stevenson's delightful poem which begins: *I curtsied to the dovecote, I curtsied to the well...*

58. Formerly known as the Crystal Arcade this is the delightful approach to the castle leading from the private landing quay. Once it was filled with art treasures, fine sculptures on pedestals brought from Italy lined the walls, alas they have gone, sold when Mrs. van Raalte left the island, last seen on the quayside with labels round their necks waiting to be shipped off to the mainland salerooms. Today there are still many fine ancient stone tablets on the walls, coats of arms and fragments of Italian sculpture set off by the Venetian pink of the walls, and always lovely flowers to give a delightful ambience of days past.

59. This striking view from a castle window looks across the gardens to Poole and Sandbanks. How many crowned and uncrowned heads of the Royal houses of Europe must have looked on this selfsame scene? For during the ownership of the van Raalte's Brownsea Castle was filled with distinguished visitors. The island was especially loved by the young Spanish princes and by Queen Marie of Rumania and her sister.

60. A corner of the gardens of Brownsea Castle. In Edwardian days a glasshouse ran the length of one wall to provide flowers and pot plants for the house. When the 1920's passed and the castle changed hands the gardens were sadly neglected, weeds and brambles ran riot for many years. How pleasant it is to see these lovely gardens restored to their original order and serenity under the care of the John Lewis Partnership, whose members use the castle for holidays. The clock tower in the background was built by Colonel Waugh above the quaint gatehouse leading to the castle.

61. The delightful old Gazebo in the gardens of Brownsea Castle. This sheltered retreat looks across the bay to Sandbanks and beyond. These charming Follies were very popular in the 19th century, they always commanded a fine view of the surrounding countryside and were protected from the winds.

62. The beautiful little church of St. Mary the Virgin on Brownsea Island was built by Colonel P. Waugh and consecrated in 1854. The islanders went to evensong here every Sunday afternoon, and afterwards, during the ownership of Mr. and Mrs. van Raalte they would all be given tea on the terrace of the castle or in the Home Field. After Mrs. van Raalte left the island in 1925 and it was later sold, the church fell into a sorry state, it was completely neglected. The fine old carvings and woodwork hidden beneath a coating of mould and grime, ivy and brambles were everywhere, peacocks wandered in and out at will. Today, how wonderful it is to see the restoration that has been carried out with loving care by many voluntary helpers, particularly from St. Peter' Church, Parkstone. It is now a place of peace and beauty.

63. Beside St. Mary's churchyard stands this fine well-head, it marks the family tomb of the Cavendish-Bentinck's. Brought from Italy by the Hon. George Cavendish-Bentinck who bought the island in 1887. He was a collector and connoisseur of Italian heraldic work, and several pieces of his collection remain on the island.

64. The Brownsea Island Estate Band, formed during the island ownership of Mr. and Mrs. van Raalte. The band consisted of workers on the island, they were all required to play an instrument, and when being interviewed they were always asked what instrument they could play. The band would entertain guests on the castle terrace during dinner. The van Raaltes designed and provided very attractive uniforms of blue and red for the bandsmen, they also bought all the instruments. This band was in demand for many events in Poole, also in various other parts of Dorset, they continued up to the outbreak of the First World War.

65. A busy scene in the harbour, crammed with vessels of every size. There is a splendid view of the Custom House with the Town Beam in front. We also see the Harbour Office, a gracious building, once a club for sea captains and merchants, erected in 1727 when Benjamin Skutt was Mayor. There is a memorial tablet to him, with his likeness in bas-relief. The colonnade was added in 1822.

66. The portrait of a remarkable man, Mr. Jesse Carter, 1830-1927. This likeness is dated about 1875, he was a man of tremendous vision and energy, having bought the pottery works in 1873 he proceeded to make many extensions, and by 1881 the pottery was on a firm footing and Jesse took into partnership his three youngest sons, Ernest Blake, Charles and Owen. Since Roman times pottery had been made in this area, evidence has been established of a small Roman pottery at Hamworthy. The Dorset ball clay deposits are considered to be amongst the finest in the world.

67. This lime kiln, circa 1874, stood on land leased from Poole Corporation, it was adjacent to the tile works. Stone from Swanage quarries was brought across the harbour in barges to be burnt in the kiln and sold as caustic lime to farmers in the hinterland of Dorset. Early one morning the buildings surrounding the kiln caught fire. The Fire Brigade was sent for, but the horses to pull the fire engine were not immediately available, and it was some time before the brigade reached the blazing scene. In the meantime fishermen formed a bucket chain to bring water from the harbour. The kiln was never rebuilt, but the base has survived and it is incorporated into the present-day Pottery as a feature for visitors.

68. A group photograph taken at Carter & Co., Poole Factory, June 1913. All were employed in the Faience Section. A highly specialised form of work, much of it is brighly glazed, it is a striking feature of two well-known factories the Pyrene and the Hoover on the Great West Road approaching London. The Firestone factory (believed to be a listed building) was recently demolished. Other outstanding work from Poole is the bandstand and the colonade at Eastbourne.

69. In a kiln at Hamworthy, the men are stacking Saggers, the boxes used for tiles or pottery. This unusual photograph shows the fine brickwork within the kiln, and the precarious nature of the work.

70. The original Fish Shambles or Market, with the Pottery chimneys and kilns in the background. The branch line in the foreground ran from Poole Railway Station, it carried Cornish clay and coal, and Dorset ball clay to the potteries.

71. The frontage of Poole Pottery circa 1910. The long wall facing the quay is much as we see it today, it was built after the reclamation of land for the quay frontage. The wall incorporated quantities of tiles and waste material, cemented together with black mortar to Jesse Carter's own recipe. The roof was covered with floor tiles set in pitch, this proved exceedingly heavy, and sagging areas were supported by increasing numbers of pit props.

72. This photograph taken in 1904 is of particular interest as it shows the craftsmen working on intricate patterns of Faience work, they are doing the actual modelling of this fine work, which may be seen in many parts of the world to which it has been exported from Poole. It was used intensively in the early years of this century in the construction of frontages for shops, hotels and public houses.

73. Tile presses being worked. At the turn of the century floor tiles were in great demand for the expanding areas of residential and business premises. Tiles from Poole were highly thought of, the plain floor tiles which included 'Carter's Red' were first made at East Quay, and subsequently at the Architectural Pottery, Hamworthy, after it was acquired by Carter's — in 1895, and where this photograph was taken. Carter's owned the red clay beds at Corfe Mullen. One of the artists who purchased blank tiles, bowls and dishes was William De Morgan whose beautifully decorated ware is highly prized by todays collectors.

74. A close-up of men stacking saggers in a biscuit kiln, Hamworthy. Saggers are open fired clay boxes into which dust-pressed and dried clay tiles are placed before being stacked and 'fired' in the kiln. The firing process takes about a week, after which the biscuit tile emerges from the saggers hard and fit for the glazing and decorating operations that follow.

75. Craftsmen modelling Faience 1904, in the Poole factory. It is a variety of majolica usually highly decorated and glazed. This is a very old method originated in Faenza, Italy in 1299. In France the name was given to certain enamelled wares made during the 16th century.

76. A scene familiar to many potters. After the shape has been 'thrown' on the potters's wheel it is put on a lathe and the base is made true by turning off some of the clay to make a foot. The craftsman is Jimmy Soper, here seen as a young man at his work. It is interesting to know that he was demonstrating his craft at Poole well beyond his normal retirement age.

77. Decorating a pot with brushwork is Ruth Pavely, who painted in a spirited manner with a light touch, following the tradition of the Delft in-glaze painting technique, which first came to England from the Netherlands in the 16th century. On completion the pieces are fired for the second time. Ruth worked at Poole Pottery from 1922 until her retirement.

78. A beautiful picture of concentration by Gertie Gilham as she 'throws' a pot made entirely by hand. The throwing wheel is probably the oldest of mechanical contrivances, and it is still used for the finest pottery, for it gives a pleasing artistic quality to the finished shape. Gertie Gilham was well-known for her artistic work.

79. Setting the finished glazed ware in the kiln ready for firing is very skilled work. After firing every piece is carefully examined and if it has the minutest flaw it is discarded. At the time this photograph was taken biscuit firing reached a temperature of 1160° and glaze firing 1050°.

80. The final stage, packers are here seen nailing down the barrels of tiles and pottery, ready for despatch. Tiles were packed in straw, and a pile of tiles may be seen waiting to be packed, whilst another pile is seen being carried forward. Coopers were employed at the factory for this work; old beer barrels were also used as seen in the foreground. For deliveries throughout the West Country of china and pottery items, large square wooden crates were used, the packing again was straw, and these could often be seen being unpacked in the roadway outside shops.

81. A portrait of Cyril Carter 1888-1969. Cyril Carter, who had become a director of Carter & Co., Ltd., in 1920, had joined that firm in 1905, and had been in the army from 1914 to 1919. He took a keen interest in the development of Carter, Stabler and Adams (now Poole Pottery Ltd.,) when it was founded in 1921, and it was largely due to his encouragement that the new venture made such rapid strides. As the link between the new subsidiary and the parent company it was his advocacy that secured the finance for each new stage of expansion. He had a keen sense of quality and artistic values that could be relied upon.

82. There are many small lakes dispersed over Wareham Heath, these were formerly old clay pits. The Blue Pool is the most well-known for its beautiful blue colour, caused by the finely suspended particles of clay, especially brilliant in the sunshine. The setting is delightful with many trees, shrubs, and sand, making a background for the startling blue of the water. A visit here is a favourite drive from Poole.

83. A lovely stretch of the river Frome as it flows on its peaceful way to Poole harbour and the sea. In the background may be seen the town of Wareham; the Church of Lady St. Mary stands behind the Priory, an old Tudor house with a garden down to the river, and wild heathland stretches into the Purbeck Hills beyond. At one time Wareham was a very busy port, but with the silting up of the river Frome it can now only be visited by smaller craft, thus it has become a charming backwater.

84. A splendid photograph of the 4th Volunteer Battalion Hants Regiment as they marched through Fordingbridge. The card is postmarked JU.15 1905 with the date stamp 304 in horizontal lines. The writer says the Battalion had marched through on the previous Tuesday when this photograph was taken. Note the George Inn sign and on the other side of the road high up on the brick wall the advertisement reads 'Good Stabling'. The army uniforms are of especial interest, as are the costumes of the watching crowd.

85. With a multitude of bell tents in the background we see a Church Parade for the 1st Volunteer Battalion Hants Regiment at Lulworth Camp 1906. The clergymen taking the service may be seen in the centre of the field, with the Regimental Band in attendance.

86. A rare photograph of the 1st Volunteer Battalion Hants Regiment on their arrival at Wool, 1906, accompanied by the regimental band. Many young men from Poole were in this regiment, as was my father, Ralph Schofield.

87. An amusing postcard sent from Poole to my father, who was with the 1st Hants Cycle Corps.

88. A portrait of Mrs. Maud Schofield née Jewell, the author's mother, whose collection of old picture postcards and photographs form a large part of this book. Wherever they happened to be, friends and relatives would send her postcards for her collection, all were kept in albums for future generations to enjoy.

89. All those who have read Thomas Hardy's works will know and love this cottage where he was born, at Higher Bockhampton, on the edge of Puddletown Heath, Hardy called it 'Egdon Heath'. As you see it is an old thatched cottage with cross beams and latticed windows. Opposite the cottage on the edge of wild moorland is a granite obelisk with the inscription: *Erected by a few American admirers in 1931*.

90. An impressive statue of a 19th century lifeboat man gazing out to sea, stands at the entrance of the Royal National Lifeboat Institution Headquarters in West Quay Road, Poole. This is the hub of the great lifeboat service around our coast, a fleet of different classes of boat of various ages, widely spread to cover the coasts of the British Isles and Ireland, all needing special equipment and stores, often at immediate notice. The depot is alongside RNLI headquarters, it has two sections to support the lifeboat fleet, the stores and the workshops. The work of these dedicated men and women leads to one end – the saving of life at sea.

91. The boathouse on Poole Quay, this is the old lifeboathouse at Fisherman's Wharf. Today it houses the 'Thomas Kirk Wright' which is on permanent loan to the Royal National Lifeboat Institution from the National Maritime Museum. The boathouse is open to visitors at certain times of the year.

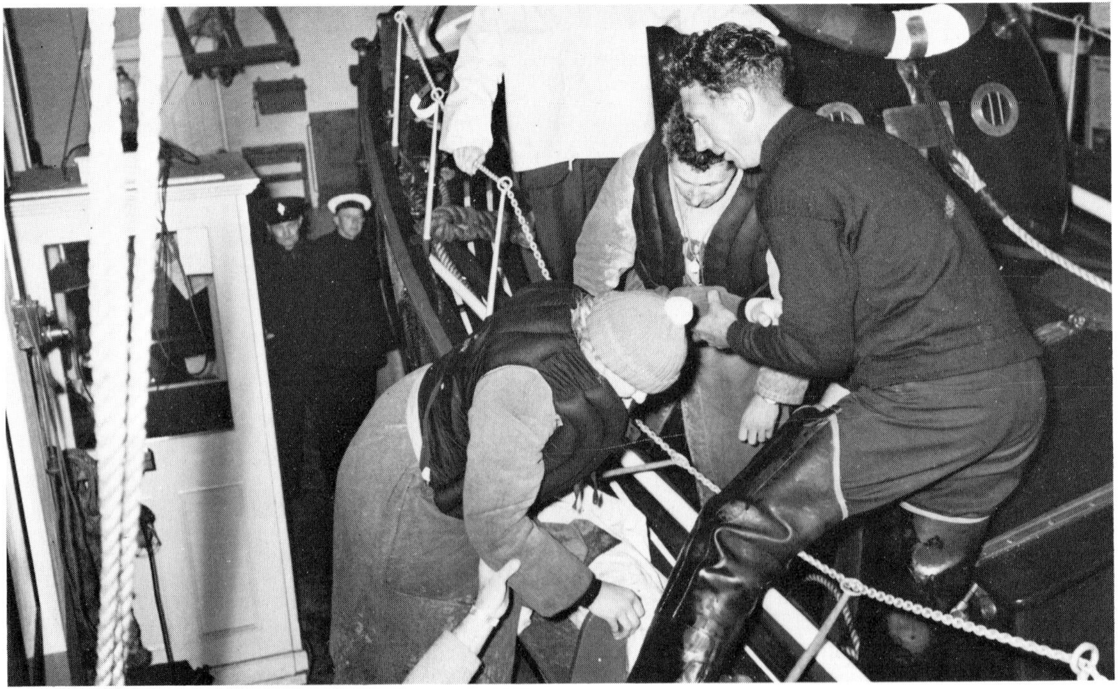

92. A dramatic moment in the boathouse after a rescue by the lifeboatmen of Poole. Survivors are seen disembarking from the lifeboat the 'Thomas Kirk Wright'. This fine lifeboat has many brave rescues to its credit and it may be seen today housed in the boathouse at Fisherman's Wharf.

93. A scene in Poole harbour showing lifeboatmen recovering the Atlantic 21 lifeboat after a demonstration launch during one of Poole Lifeboat Open Days. These are always popular events as may be seen from the large crowd gathered.

94. A busy scene in the RNLI workshops showing the skilled craftsmen making some of the equipment needed for the lifeboat fleet. Here men have worked overnight to repair parts of a lifeboat that has come in badly damaged. They often work against the clock, in order to keep the boats fully seaworthy to meet all emergencies.

95. A dramatic night scene with a happy ending. The Poole lifeboat is leaving Wareham after safely landing a rescued boy. Just one of the many hundreds of successful rescues made by the crew of the lifeboat.

96. A splendid photograph of coxswain Richard H. Hayes of Poole. He was coxswain of the Poole lifeboat from March 1931 to June 1946, during which time there were two lifeboats, the 'RNLB Hamar' on station from 1919 to 1939 when she launched on service 40 times and saved 60 lives. The second lifeboat the 'RNLB THOMAS KIRK WRIGHT' on station from 1939 to 1962, during which time she launched on service 64 times saving 15 lives.

97. The 20 feet Boston Whaler ‘Outrage’, at one time stationed at Poole and replacing a 17 feet ‘Dell Quay Dory’. She is the only boat of this type in the RNLI fleet, she has a crew of three, a maximum speed of 30 knots and an endurance at full speed of six hours.

98. A postcard from Edwardian days showing this wild and dramatic coast, the scene of many wrecks, and from where ships make a run for Poole harbour to escape the storms. It is a cruel coast for ships and the men who sail them. The tale is told of the ghostly pealing of bells off Handfast Point during a gale, said to come from a ship that sank off the Point, amongst its cargo it carried bells for a Poole church.

99. The Old Harry Rocks off Handfast Point, at the southern end of Studland Bay, as they stood before the severe gale of 1896, when 'Old Harry' was badly damaged, and his 'Wife' even more so, being reduced to a mere stump from the battering of wind and waves. But still 'Old Harry' stands, in proud defiance of the elements, a famous landmark shining white in the sunlight, and ghostly luminous by moonlight.

100. A pleasant drive from Poole is a visit to Swanage, a quiet corner of Dorset with its old inns and cottages, the seafront extends for almost three-quarters of a mile. In Victorian times much marble and stone was quarried in the nearby hills, and shipped from the old pier, only a few pieces of the structure now remain. On the esplanade a granite column bears the inscription: *In commemoration of a great Naval battle fought with the Danes by Alfred the Great A.D. 877.*

101. The Great Globe is one of the principal sights to visit in the area. It stands on Durlston Head, cut out of eight blocks of stone and placed here by Mr. George Burt, who came from a quarrying family and was a member of the firm of Mowlem & Co. I well remember as a small girl being brought from Poole to see this enormous stone model. The stone tablets in the background bear the date 1891, and give information on the earth, the sun, moon and stars, also several quotations from the bible under the inscription 'God the Creator and Ruler of the Universe'.

102. The famous Tilly Whim Caves, near Anvil Point, today a popular tourist attraction. On the hills around may be seen many surface workings of the quarries, mostly owned and worked for generations by local families. There is a variety of colour in the stone, shades of grey, sometimes creamy, this stone was extracted close to the surface. These caves are no longer worked.

103. The ancient Chapel of St. Catherine, Abbotsbury, had a long period of neglect until it was restored in 1907. The chapel is dedicated to St. Catherine of Alexandria since it stands on a hill-top, as were many churches dedicated to her, she is said to have been buried by angels on Mount Sinai. The patron saint of spinsters her day is still celebrated by the midinettes of Paris, with the chant: *St. Catherine, St. Catherine, O lend me thine aid, And grant that I never may die an old maid.*

104. The mediaeval village of Corfe with its castle dominating the scene. The grey stone walled cottages are very picturesque, over some of the doorways are stones engraved by the famous Purbeck marblers. On Shrove Tuesday the Ancient Order of Marblers and Stonecutters meet in the Town Hall. Time was when men brought their sons to be entered on the apprenticeship records, there was a tradition that the new apprentice had to make a dash across the road holding a pint of beer in his hand, whilst others would try to prevent him reaching the other side. They also kicked a football along a track across the heath to present the ball and a pound of pepper at Ower Farm, then crossing Ower Heath to Ower Quay, it was from this spot that Purbeck marble was shipped to Poole, today only the landing stage remains.

105. At the centre of the charming little village of Corfe lies the Square, with its attractive old inns and cottages. In the background may be seen the 14th century Cross, with a shaft and a cross commemorating Queen Victoria's Diamond Jubilee. The roof tiles are especially pleasing, as is the warm and weathered brick of the Museum and the Town Hall.

106. Corfe Castle showing what a formidable fortress it once was, as we look up the steep hill from the village of Corfe. A favourite place to visit from Poole the castle can be seen from miles around. It has been established that Elfrida, widow of King Edgar, owned a hunting-lodge here in 978. The castle has many legends that have been handed down through the ages. William the Conqueror ordered the building of the castle about 1080 and this continued during the next 200 years. Today the ancient ruins are an impressive sight.

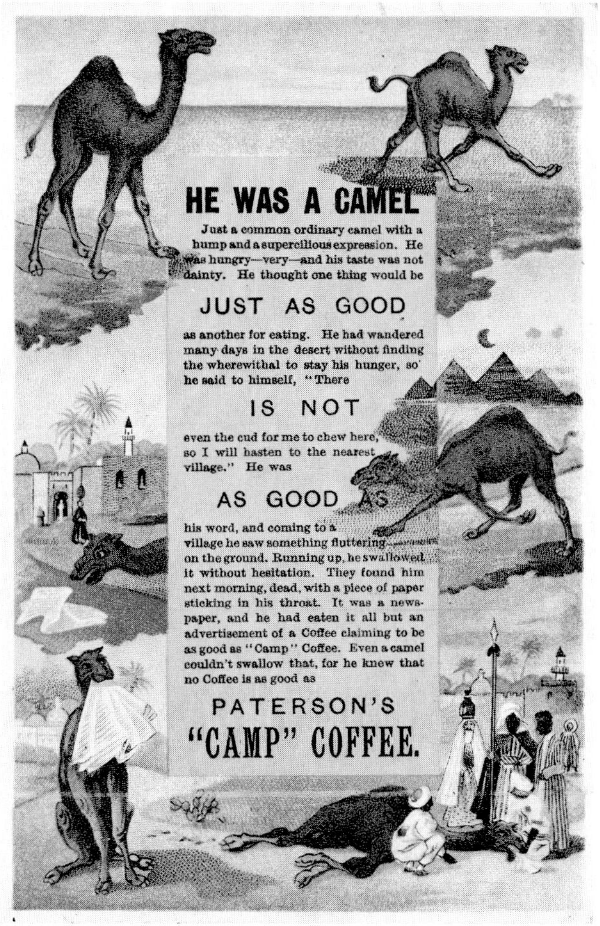

107. An amusing card postmarked Poole, 9-15p.m.1904. One might add 'and still going strong'.

108. Lulworth Castle lies in a beautiful setting of trees and green pastures. A pleasant drive from Poole it lies on the road to the Cove. This once fine castle was built in 1610, the four distinctive towers remain, but within it is a ruin having suffered a terrible fire in 1929. Brick built and faced with Purbeck and Portland stone from the area it has a fortress-like appearance. After landing at Poole on 16th August 1830 came Charles X of France to find refuge here. On seeing the castle he is said to have exclaimed: 'Voilà, la Bastille.'

LULWORTH COVE 558

109. Beautiful Lulworth Cove as it will be remembered by many, a renowned beauty spot, the small bay is enclosed by steep cliffs. The area is a geologists paradise with many unusual rock formations, Stair Hole a natural chasm into which the sea rushes at high tide, and at South Rocks the fascinating remains of a fossilised forest.

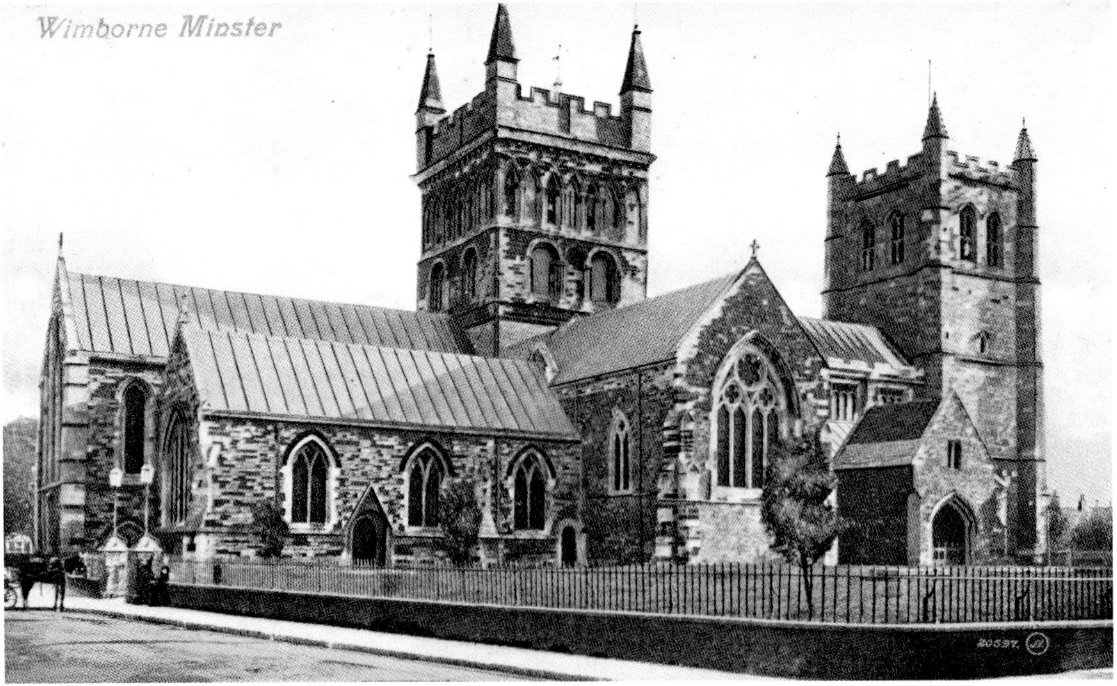

110. Many a pilgrimage was made to Wimborne Minster as long as a thousand years ago, for it was the home of Kings, and here lies the great Saxon King Ethelred. Not long after the Conquest the present church was built. Since that time many additons have been made, but each architect has endeavoured to preserve the fine features of the original building.

111. The Grammar School, Wimborne, the postcard was sent from Parkstone in June 1906. The uniform of the boys is of particular interest as they play a game of cricket. This fine old listed building has now been converted and restored into private houses of different sizes, but still retaining the original charming façade. Each of the houses has been named after a former headmaster of the school since 1822.

112. This curious card is postmarked Oc.8.1907, it pictures the Quarter Jack as it is known, and it stands high on the north side of the western tower of Wimborne Minster. It is the wooden figure of a man, originally a monk, but here dressed in the style of a British Grenadier of the Napoleonic era. On either side of the figure are bells which strike the quarters.

113. In the north choir aisle of Wimbore Minster is this ancient Saxon chest, which is thought to have been in use in St. Cuthburga's Church, and may have been used to store relics. Another very old chest in this aisle has six locks and contains the deeds of charity lands, each of the six trustees had a key to the chest, a third chest holds the parish accounts from 1475.

Rufus Stone, Nr. Lyndhurst, New Forest.
Howard's Series, 300.

114. To wander in the New Forest is a delight not found elsewhere. The Rufus Stone was placed here by Earl De la Warr in 1745. Old traditions have given varying accounts of the death of King William II at this spot. The inscription on the stone, which was encased in an iron cover in 1841 reads: *Here stood the old tree on which an arrow shot by Sir Walter Tyrrell at a stag glanced off and struck King William the Second, surnamed Rufus, on the breast, of which he instantly died. On the second day of August Anno 1100.*

115. Near the Rufus Stone, in the New Forest, is this curiosity of nature, a double tree of oak and beech. Once riding here in the early morning with the forest silent and mysterious, and patches of mist still hanging in the trees, we came upon a tiny sleeping foal with its mare standing guard over it, the mare did not move, but just glanced in our direction as we turned our horses so as not to disturb this perfect scene.

DOUBLE TREE. Oak and Beech, near Rufus Stone.
Howard's Series, No. 316.

116. An idyllic cameo of a forest scene near Lyndhurst Road. A lovely drive from Poole for picnics and walks, as popular today as it was at the turn of the century. A place of peace and tranquility, 'far from the madding crowd'. Postmarked 1906.

117. The Priory Church, Christchurch, is one of the finest in England. Here we see the solid building of the Normans, and examples of many styles of architecture from Early English in the crypt, to the Renaissance of the chantries. The story of the foundation of the church is mixed with fact and legend. This beautiful Norman church was begun at the end of the 11th century by Roger Flambard, he had great ability and energy and had risen in the time of Rufus from being superintendent of the King's kitchens to the position of Chancellor, Treasurer and Bishop of Durham.

OLD TOWN BRIDGE AND PRIORY, CHRISTCHURCH. 58

118. This is one of the most beautiful views of Christchurch Priory showing the Old Town Bridge, with the river peacefully flowing to the sea. Close by the Avon and the Stour rivers meet on their way to Christchurch Bay.

119. The Priory with its great variety of architecture delights the student and the casual visitor. Many of the carvings in the durable Caen stone are so delicate that they are still as perfect today as when they were first carved. In this peep we see the magnificence of the Norman masonry, the fine arcading and the richly worked triforium.

120. A pleasing scene of Priory Avenue postmarked 1903. From Saxon times there was a church and a town at the estuary of the Avon and the Stour rivers. In the Domesday Book the church is called Holy Trinity, and the town had the name of Twynham, 'between the waters'.

121. This idyllic scene was sent from Poole in 1904. It shows the peaceful Talbot Woods, named after the founder of Talbot Village, Miss Georgina Charlotte Talbot of Hinton Wood House, Bournemouth. The village consisted of small farms, five in number, about twenty cottages, a church, a school and seven endowed almshouses.

THE INVALIDS WALK, BOURNEMOUTH.

122. Well-known to many visitors the Invalids Walk, Bournemouth, with its tall pines and restful air is a pleasant place to stroll. This postcard sent in 1906 shows the ladies costume of the day, ground length skirt and tight waist and the straw hat probably laden with flowers and fruit. The message reads: *The tram rides are fine here but a bit dear, one penny a mile.*

123. A last look at Poole Quay. The old buildings have always attracted artists in oils and water colours, they paint away at the quayside, whilst the busy life of this working harbour goes on as it has done for centuries. It must have been a rare sight to see the fleet of windjammers sailing out of the harbour, or coming home from the high seas laden with goods from China, the Indies, Newfoundland and the Mediterranean ports.

124. A suitable end to this collection is the splendid photograph of Frank Ide, the present coxswain of the Poole lifeboat 'Inner Wheel'. He personifies the grit and determination of Poole past, with the forward looking endeavour of Poole present.